This journal belongs to

Belle City Gifts™
Savage, MN

Belle City Gifts is an imprint of BroadStreet Publishing
Broadstreetpublishing.com

Delight yourself in the Lord
© 2020 by BroadStreet Publishing®

978-1-4245-6081-3

Edited by Michelle Winger I literallyprecise.com.
Design by Chris Garborg I garborgdesign.com.

Printed in China.

20 21 22 23 24   5 4 3 2 1

Delight
Yourself
in the
Lord

Abandonment

The Lord himself goes before you and will be with you;
he will never leave you nor forsake you.

Deuteronomy 31:8 NIV

Those who know your name trust in you,
for you, O Lord, do not abandon
those who search for you.

Psalm 9:10 NLT

God made my life complete
when I placed all the pieces before him....
God rewrote the text of my life
when I opened the book of my heart to his eyes.

Psalm 18:20, 24 MSG

I will bring the blind by a way they did not know;
I will lead them in paths they have not known.
I will make darkness light before them,
And crooked places straight.
These things will I do for them,
And not forsake them.

Isaiah 42:16 NKJV

The Lord will not abandon His people on account of
His great name, because the Lord has been pleased to
make you a people for Himself.

1 Samuel 12:22 NASB

"I will not abandon you as orphans—I will come to you."

John 14:18 NLT

Abuse

The LORD is near to the brokenhearted
and saves the crushed in spirit.

Psalm 34:18 ESV

LORD , you know the hopes of the helpless.
Surely you will hear their cries and comfort them.
You will bring justice to the orphans and the oppressed,
so mere people can no longer terrify them.

Psalm 10:17–18 NLT

The LORD hears his people
when they call to him for help.
He rescues them from all their troubles.

Psalm 34:17 NLT

You, God, see the trouble of the afflicted;
you consider their grief and take it in hand.
The victims commit themselves to you;
you are the helper of the fatherless.

Psalm 10:14 NIV

We're not giving up. How could we! Even though on the
outside it often looks like things are falling apart on us,
on the inside, where God is making new life, not a day
goes by without his unfolding grace.

2 Corinthians 4:16 MSG

You, O LORD, are a shield about me,
My glory, and the One who lifts my head.

Psalm 3:3 NASB

Acceptance

I've redeemed you.
I've called your name. You're mine.
When you're in over your head, I'll be there with you.
When you're in rough waters, you will not go down.
When you're between a rock and a hard place,
it won't be a dead end—
Because I am GOD, your personal God,
The Holy of Israel, your Savior.
I paid a huge price for you...!
That's how much you mean to me!
That's how much I love you!

Isaiah 43:1–4 MSG

If God is for us, who can be against us?

Romans 8:31 ESV

"The Father gives me the people who are mine. Every one of them will come to me, and I will always accept them."

John 6:37 NCV

"Here I am! I stand at the door and knock. If anyone hears my voice and opens the door, I will come in and eat with that person, and they with me."

Revelation 3:20 NIV

Before he made the world, God chose us to be his very own through what Christ would do for us; he decided then to make us holy in his eyes, without a single fault— we who stand before him covered with his love.

Ephesians 1:4 TLB

Addiction

No temptation has overtaken you except what is common to mankind. And God is faithful; he will not let you be tempted beyond what you can bear. But when you are tempted, he will also provide a way out so that you can endure it.

1 Corinthians 10:13 NIV

Abstain from the passions of the flesh, which wage war against your soul.

1 Peter 2:11 ESV

Give your bodies to God because of all he has done for you. Let them be a living and holy sacrifice—the kind he will find acceptable. This is truly the way to worship him.

Romans 12:1 NLT

It was for freedom that Christ set us free; therefore keep standing firm and do not be subject again to a yoke of slavery.

Galatians 5:1 NASB

Anyone who belongs to Christ has become a new person. The old life is gone; a new life has begun!

2 Corinthians 5:17 NLT

Submit to God. Resist the devil and he will flee from you.

James 4:7 NKJV

"If the Son sets you free, you will be free indeed."

John 8:36 NIV

Anger

Everyone should be quick to listen, slow to speak and slow to become angry, because human anger does not produce the righteousness that God desires.

James 1:19–20 NIV

Whatever is true, whatever is noble, whatever is right, whatever is pure, whatever is lovely, whatever is admirable—if anything is excellent or praiseworthy—think about such things.

Philippians 4:8 NIV

Whoever is slow to anger has great understanding.

Proverbs 14:29 ESV

Don't let evil get the best of you; get the best of evil by doing good.

Romans 12:21 MSG

A fool vents all his feelings,
But a wise man holds them back.

Proverbs 29:11 NKJV

"In your anger do not sin": Do not let the sun go down while you are still angry, and do not give the devil a foothold.

Ephesians 4:26–27 NIV

Be not quick in your spirit to become angry,
for anger lodges in the heart of fools.

Ecclesiastes 7:9 ESV

Anxiety

Cast all your anxiety on him because he cares for you.

1 Peter 5:7 NIV

Do not be anxious about anything, but in every situation, by prayer and petition, with thanksgiving, present your requests to God.

Philippians 4:6 NIV

"Trusting me, you will be unshakable and assured, deeply at peace. In this godless world you will continue to experience difficulties. But take heart! I've conquered the world."

John 16:33 MSG

In my trouble I cried to the LORD,
And He answered me.

Psalm 120:1 NASB

"Let not your heart be troubled. You are trusting God, now trust in me."

John 14:1 TLB

If you make the LORD your refuge,
if you make the Most High your shelter,
no evil will conquer you;
no plague will come near your home.
For he will order his angels
to protect you wherever you go.

Psalm 91:9–11 NLT

Beauty

Don't be concerned about the outward beauty of
fancy hairstyles, expensive jewelry, or beautiful clothes.
You should clothe yourselves instead with the beauty
that comes from within, the unfading beauty of a
gentle and quiet spirit, which is so precious to God.

1 Peter 3:3–4 NLT

I will praise You,
for I am fearfully and wonderfully made;
Marvelous are Your works,
And that my soul knows very well.

Psalm 139:14 NKJV

"Has anyone by fussing in front of the mirror ever
gotten taller by so much as an inch? All this time and
money wasted on fashion—do you think it makes that
much difference? Instead of looking at the fashions,
walk out into the fields and look at the wildflowers.
They never primp or shop, but have you ever seen color
and design quite like it? The ten best-dressed men and
women in the country look shabby alongside them."

Matthew 6:27–29 MSG

The LORD doesn't see things the way you see them.
People judge by outward appearance, but the LORD
looks at the heart.

1 Samuel 16:7 NLT

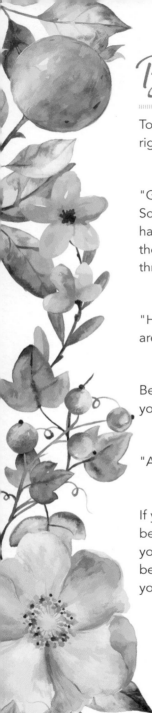

Belief

To all who did accept him and believe in him he gave the right to become children of God.

John 1:12 NCV

"God so loved the world that he gave his one and only Son, that whoever believes in him shall not perish but have eternal life. For God did not send his Son into the world to condemn the world, but to save the world through him. Whoever believes in him is not condemned."

John 3:16-18 NIV

"Have you believed because you have seen me? Blessed are those who have not seen and yet have believed."

John 20:29 ESV

Believe on the Lord Jesus Christ, and you will be saved, you and your household.

Acts 16:31 NKJV

"Anything is possible if a person believes."

Mark 9:23 NLT

If you declare with your mouth, "Jesus is Lord," and believe in your heart that God raised him from the dead, you will be saved. For it is with your heart that you believe and are justified, and it is with your mouth that you profess your faith and are saved.

Romans 10:9-10 NIV

Blessings

Blessed be the God and Father of our Lord Jesus Christ, who has blessed us in Christ with every spiritual blessing in the heavenly places, even as he chose us in him before the foundation of the world, that we should be holy and blameless before him.

Ephesians 1:3–4 ESV

You prepare a feast for me
in the presence of my enemies.
You honor me by anointing my head with oil.
My cup overflows with blessings.

Psalm 23:5 NLT

Taste and see that the LORD is good;
blessed is the one who takes refuge in him!

Psalm 34:8 NIV

The LORD bless you, and keep you;
The LORD make His face shine on you,
And be gracious to you;
The LORD lift up His countenance on you,
And give you peace.

Numbers 6:24–26 NASB

How blessed all those in whom you live,
whose lives become roads you travel;
They wind through lonesome valleys, come upon brooks,
discover cool springs and pools brimming with rain!

Psalm 84:5–6 MSG

Caring

Bear one another's burdens, and so fulfill the law of Christ.

Galatians 6:2 ESV

If anyone has material possessions and sees a brother or sister in need but has no pity on them, how can the love of God be in that person? Dear children, let us not love with words or speech but with actions and in truth.

1 John 3:17–18 NIV

Do not merely look out for your own personal interests, but also for the interests of others.

Philippians 2:4 NASB

"I was hungry and you gave me something to eat, I was thirsty and you gave me something to drink, I was a stranger and you invited me in, I needed clothes and you clothed me, I was sick and you looked after me, I was in prison and you came to visit me.... Whatever you did for one of the least of these brothers and sisters of mine, you did for me."

Matthew 25:35–36, 40 NIV

Pure and genuine religion in the sight of God the Father means caring for orphans and widows in their distress.

James 1:27 NLT

Change

Our faces, then, are not covered. We all show the Lord's glory, and we are being changed to be like him. This change in us brings ever greater glory, which comes from the Lord, who is the Spirit.

2 Corinthians 3:18 NCV

"Unless you change and become like little children, you will never enter the kingdom of heaven."

Matthew 18:3 NIV

Jesus Christ is the same yesterday and today and forever.

Hebrews 13:8 NASB

He will take our weak mortal bodies and change them into glorious bodies like his own, using the same power with which he will bring everything under his control.

Philippians 3:21 NLT

We shall not all sleep, but we shall all be changed.

1 Corinthians 15:51 NKJV

Every good gift and every perfect gift is from above, coming down from the Father of lights with whom there is no variation or shadow due to change.

James 1:17 ESV

There is a time for everything, and everything on earth has its special season.

Ecclesiastes 3:1 NCV

Commitment

Stand firm. Let nothing move you. Always give yourselves fully to the work of the Lord, because you know that your labor in the Lord is not in vain.

1 Corinthians 15:58 NIV

"If any of you wants to be my follower, you must turn from your selfish ways, take up your cross daily, and follow me."

Luke 9:23 NLT

Commit your work to the LORD,
and your plans will be established.

Proverbs 16:3 ESV

"Seek first the kingdom of God and His righteousness, and all these things shall be added to you."

Matthew 6:33 NKJV

Commit everything you do to the LORD.
Trust him, and he will help you.

Psalm 37:5 NLT

I have fought the good fight, I have finished the course, I have kept the faith; in the future there is laid up for me the crown of righteousness, which the Lord, the righteous Judge, will award to me on that day; and not only to me, but also to all who have loved His appearing.

2 Timothy 4:7-8 NASB

Compassion

Where is another God like you, who pardons the sins
of the survivors among his people? You cannot
stay angry with your people, for you love to be merciful.
Once again you will have compassion on us. You will tread
our sins beneath your feet; you will throw them into
the depths of the ocean! You will bless us as you
promised Jacob long ago. You will set your love upon us,
as you promised our father Abraham!

Micah 7:18–20 TLB

Be gracious to me, O God,
according to Your lovingkindness;
According to the greatness of Your
compassion blot out my transgressions.

Psalm 51:1 NASB

You, O Lord, are a God full of compassion, and gracious,
Longsuffering and abundant in mercy and truth.

Psalm 86:15 NKJV

The LORD longs to be gracious to you;
therefore he will rise up to show you compassion.
For the LORD is a God of justice.
Blessed are all who wait for him!

Isaiah 30:18 NIV

Praise be to the God and Father of our Lord Jesus Christ,
the Father of compassion and the God of all comfort.

2 Corinthians 1:3 NIV

Confidence

Be my rock of refuge,
to which I can always go;
give the command to save me,
for you are my rock and my fortress....
You have been my hope, Sovereign LORD,
my confidence since my youth.

Psalm 71:3, 5 NIV

We can confidently say, "The Lord is my helper;
I will not fear; what can man do to me?"

Hebrews 13:6 ESV

I am confident of this very thing, that He who began a good
work in you will perfect it until the day of Christ Jesus.

Philippians 1:6 NASB

I can do everything through Christ, who gives me strength.

Philippians 4:13 NLT

Let us then approach God's throne of grace with confidence,
so that we may receive mercy and find grace to help us in
our time of need.

Hebrews 4:16 NIV

This is the confidence that we have toward him, that if we
ask anything according to his will he hears us. And if we
know that he hears us in whatever we ask, we know that we
have the requests that we have asked of him.

1 John 5:14–15 ESV

Contentment

"You're blessed when you're content with just who you are—no more, no less. That's the moment you find yourselves proud owners of everything that can't be bought."

Matthew 5:5 MSG

I know what it is to be in need, and I know what it is to have plenty. I have learned the secret of being content in any and every situation, whether well fed or hungry, whether living in plenty or in want. I can do all this through him who gives me strength.

Philippians 4:12-13 NIV

"If God cares so wonderfully for wildflowers that are here today and thrown into the fire tomorrow, he will certainly care for you. Why do you have so little faith? So don't worry about these things, saying, "What will we eat? What will we drink? What will we wear?" These things dominate the thoughts of unbelievers, but your heavenly Father already knows all your needs. Seek the Kingdom of God above all else, and live righteously, and he will give you everything you need."

Matthew 6:30-33 NLT

"If you're content to simply be yourself, your life will count for plenty."

Matthew 23:12 MSG

Cooperation

May the God of endurance and encouragement grant you to live in such harmony with one another, in accord with Christ Jesus, that together you may with one voice glorify the God and Father of our Lord Jesus Christ. Therefore welcome one another as Christ has welcomed you, for the glory of God.

Romans 15:5-7 ESV

I appeal to you…that all of you agree with one another in what you say and that there be no divisions among you, but that you be perfectly united in mind and thought.

1 Corinthians 1:10 NIV

Make me truly happy by agreeing wholeheartedly with each other, loving one another, and working together with one mind and purpose.

Philippians 2:2 NLT

Be harmonious, sympathetic, brotherly, kindhearted, and humble in spirit; not returning evil for evil or insult for insult, but giving a blessing instead; for you were called for the very purpose that you might inherit a blessing.

1 Peter 3:8-9 NASB

Be of the same mind toward one another. Do not set your mind on high things, but associate with the humble. Do not be wise in your own opinion.

Romans 12:16 NKJV

Courage

Be strong and courageous. Do not be frightened,
and do not be dismayed, for the LORD your God is
with you wherever you go.

Joshua 1:9 ESV

Love the LORD, all you godly ones!
For the LORD protects those who are loyal to him,
but he harshly punishes the arrogant.
So be strong and courageous,
all you who put your hope in the LORD!

Psalm 31:23–24 NLT

Be strong in the Lord and in his mighty power.
Put on the full armor of God, so that you can
take your stand against the devil's schemes.

Ephesians 6:10–11 NIV

Even though I walk through the valley
of the shadow of death,
I fear no evil, for You are with me;
Your rod and Your staff, they comfort me.

Psalm 23:4 NASB

When I am afraid, I put my trust in you.
In God, whose word I praise—
in God I trust and am not afraid.

Psalm 56:3–4 NIV

Be on guard. Stand firm in the faith. Be courageous.
Be strong. And do everything with love.

1 Corinthians 16:13–14 NLT

Courtesy

Seek to do good to one another and to everyone.

1 Thessalonians 5:15 ESV

We who are strong must be considerate of those who are sensitive about things.... We must not just please ourselves. We should help others do what is right and build them up in the Lord. For even Christ didn't live to please himself.

Romans 15:1–3 NLT

Do a favor and win a friend forever;
nothing can untie that bond.
Words satisfy the mind as much as fruit does the stomach;
good talk is as gratifying as a good harvest.
Words kill, words give life;
they're either poison or fruit—you choose.

Proverbs 18:19–21 MSG

Let your speech always be with grace, as though seasoned with salt, so that you will know how you should respond to each person.

Colossians 4:6 NASB

Do not forget to show hospitality to strangers, for by so doing some people have shown hospitality to angels without knowing it.

Hebrews 13:2 NIV

Remind them...to be obedient, to be ready for every good work, to speak evil of no one, to avoid quarreling, to be gentle, and to show perfect courtesy toward all people.

Titus 3:1–2 ESV

Creativity

The whole earth is filled with awe at your wonders.

Psalm 65:8 NIV

We are God's masterpiece. He has created us anew in Christ Jesus, so we can do the good things he planned for us long ago.

Ephesians 2:10 NLT

The heavens are telling of the glory of God;
And their expanse is declaring the work of His hands.

Psalm 19:1 NASB

You created my inmost being;
you knit me together in my mother's womb.
I praise you because I am fearfully and wonderfully made;
your works are wonderful,
I know that full well.

Psalm 139:13-14 NIV

O Lord, what a variety of things you have made!
In wisdom you have made them all.
The earth is full of your creatures.

Psalm 104:24 NLT

Having then gifts differing according to the grace that is given to us, let us use them.

Romans 12:6 NKJV

Depression

Whatever is true, whatever is honorable, whatever is just, whatever is pure, whatever is lovely, whatever is commendable, if there is any excellence, if there is anything worth of praise, think about these things..

Philippians 4:8 ESV

The LORD hears his people
when they call to him for help.
He rescues them from all their troubles.

Psalm 34:17 NLT

He has delivered us from the power of darkness and conveyed us into the kingdom of the Son of His love.

Colossians 1:13 NKJV

Why, my soul, are you downcast?
Why so disturbed within me?
Put your hope in God,
for I will yet praise him,
my Savior and my God.

Psalm 42:11 NIV

You, O LORD, are a shield about me,
my glory, and the lifter of my head.

Psalm 3:3 ESV

You are a chosen people, a royal priesthood, a holy nation, God's special possession, that you may declare the praises of him who called you out of darkness into his wonderful light.

1 Peter 2:9 NIV

Diligence

To enjoy your work and to accept your lot in life—that is indeed a gift from God. The person who does that will not need to look back with sorrow on his past, for God gives him joy.

Ecclesiastes 5:20 TLB

Do not neglect your gift.... Be diligent in these matters; give yourself wholly to them, so that everyone may see your progress.

1 Timothy 4:14-15 NIV

Do you see people skilled in their work?
They will work for kings, not for ordinary people.

Proverbs 22:29 NCV

Let us not get tired of doing what is right, for after a while we will reap a harvest of blessing if we don't get discouraged and give up.

Galatians 6:9 TLB

The plans of the diligent lead to profit.

Proverbs 21:5 NIV

Work with enthusiasm, as though you were working for the Lord rather than for people.

Ephesians 6:7 NLT

Wise words bring many benefits,
and hard work brings rewards.

Proverbs 12:14 NLT

Disability

God will never forget the needy;
the hope of the afflicted will never perish.

Psalm 9:18 NIV

"My grace is sufficient for you, for my power is made perfect in weakness." Therefore I will boast all the more gladly of my weaknesses, so that the power of Christ may rest upon me.

2 Corinthians 12:9 ESV

After you have suffered for a little while, the God of all grace, who called you to His eternal glory in Christ, will Himself perfect, confirm, strengthen and establish you.

1 Peter 5:10 NASB

Take a new grip with your tired hands and strengthen your weak knees. Mark out a straight path for your feet so that those who are weak and lame will not fall but become strong.

Hebrews 12:12-14 NLT

He will not break the bruised reed, nor quench the dimly burning flame. He will encourage the fainthearted, those tempted to despair. He will see full justice given to all who have been wronged.

Isaiah 42:3 TLB

Consider it pure joy, my brothers and sisters, whenever you face trials of many kinds, because you know that the testing of your faith produces perseverance.

James 1:2-3 NIV

Discouragement

In all this you greatly rejoice, though now for a little while you may have had to suffer grief in all kinds of trials. These have come so that the proven genuineness of your faith—of greater worth than gold, which perishes even though refined by fire—may result in praise, glory and honor when Jesus Christ is revealed.

1 Peter 1:6–7 NIV

Do not lose the courage you had in the past, which has a great reward. You must hold on, so you can do what God wants and receive what he has promised.

Hebrews 10:35–36 NCV

We are pressed on every side by troubles, but we are not crushed. We are perplexed, but not driven to despair. We are hunted down, but never abandoned by God. We get knocked down, but we are not destroyed.

2 Corinthians 4:8–9 NLT

"Let not your heart be troubled; you believe in God, believe also in Me. In My Father's house are many mansions.... I go to prepare a place for you. And if I go and prepare a place for you, I will come again and receive you to Myself; that where I am, there you may be also."

John 14:1-3 NKJV

Encouragement

Let everything you say be good and helpful, so that your words will be an encouragement to those who hear them.

Ephesians 4:29 NLT

We do not lose heart, but though our outer man is decaying, yet our inner man is being renewed day by day. For momentary, light affliction is producing for us an eternal weight of glory far beyond all comparison.

2 Corinthians 4:16–17 NASB

The humble will see their God at work and be glad. Let all who seek God's help be encouraged.

Psalm 69:32 NLT

We ask God to give you complete knowledge of his will and to give you spiritual wisdom and understanding. Then the way you live will always honor and please the Lord, and your lives will produce every kind of good fruit. All the while, you will grow as you learn to know God better and better.

Colossians 1:9–10 NLT

Let us consider how to stir up one another to love and good works, not neglecting to meet together, as is the habit of some, but encouraging one another.

Hebrews 10:24–25 ESV

Enthusiasm

Whatever you do, work heartily, as for the Lord
and not for men, knowing that from the Lord you
will receive the inheritance as your reward. You are
serving the Lord Christ.

Colossians 3:23–24 ESV

When I discovered your words, I devoured them.
They are my joy and my heart's delight,
for I bear your name,
O LORD God of Heaven's Armies.

Jeremiah 15:16 NLT

Make the most of every opportunity. Let your
conversation be always full of grace.

Colossians 4:5–6 NIV

You will light my lamp;
The LORD my God will enlighten my darkness.
For by You I can run against a troop,
By my God I can leap over a wall.

Psalm 18:28–29 NKJV

Oh, how sweet the light of day,
And how wonderful to live in the sunshine!
Even if you live a long time,
don't take a single day for granted.
Take delight in each light-filled hour.

Ecclesiastes 11:7–8 MSG

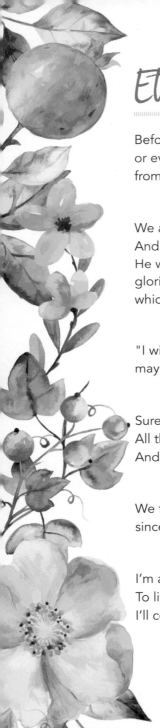

Eternity

Before the mountains were brought forth,
or ever you had formed the earth and the world,
from everlasting to everlasting you are God.

Psalm 90:2 ESV

We are citizens of heaven, where the Lord Jesus Christ lives.
And we are eagerly waiting for him to return as our Savior.
He will take our weak mortal bodies and change them into
glorious bodies like his own, using the same power with
which he will bring everything under his control.

Philippians 3:20–21 NLT

"I will come back and take you to be with me that you also
may be where I am."

John 14:3 NIV

Surely goodness and mercy shall follow me
All the days of my life;
And I will dwell in the house of the LORD Forever.

Psalm 23:6 NKJV

We fix our eyes not on what is seen, but on what is unseen,
since what is seen is temporary, but what is unseen is eternal.

2 Corinthians 4:18 NIV

I'm asking GOD for one thing, only one thing:
To live with him in his house my whole life long.
I'll contemplate his beauty; I'll study at his feet.

Psalm 27:4 MSG

Excellence

It is my prayer that your love may abound more and more, with knowledge and all discernment, so that you may approve what is excellent, and so be pure and blameless for the day of Christ.

Philippians 1:9–10 ESV

His divine power has granted to us everything pertaining to life and godliness, through the true knowledge of Him who called us by His own glory and excellence.

2 Peter 1:3 NASB

Whether you eat or drink, or whatever you do, do all to the glory of God.

1 Corinthians 10:31 NKJV

Do your best to present yourself to God as one approved, a worker who does not need to be ashamed and who correctly handles the word of truth.

2 Timothy 2:15 NIV

"Many women have done excellently,
but you surpass them all."
Charm is deceitful, and beauty is vain,
but a woman who fears the LORD is to be praised.
Give her of the fruit of her hands,
and let her works praise her in the gates.

Proverbs 31:29–31 ESV

Faith

Faith is confidence in what we hope for and assurance about what we do not see.

Hebrews 11:1 NIV

Through Christ you have come to trust in God. And you have placed your faith and hope in God because he raised Christ from the dead and gave him great glory.

1 Peter 1:21 NLT

Without faith it is impossible to please God, because anyone who comes to him must believe that he exists and that he rewards those who earnestly seek him.

Hebrews 11:6 NIV

Faith comes by hearing, and hearing by the word of God.

Romans 10:17 NKJV

"If you have faith like a grain of mustard seed, you will say to this mountain, 'Move from here to there,' and it will move, and nothing will be impossible for you."

Matthew 17:20 ESV

As we pray to our God and Father about you, we think of your faithful work, your loving deeds, and the enduring hope you have because of our Lord Jesus Christ.

1 Thessalonians 1:3 NLT

"As many as received Him, to them He gave the right to become children of God, even to those who believe in His name."

John 1:12 NASB

Faithfulness

Your lovingkindness, O Lord, extends to the heavens,
Your faithfulness reaches to the skies.

Psalm 36:5 NASB

God is faithful. He will not allow the temptation to be more
than you can stand. When you are tempted, he will show
you a way out so that you can endure.

1 Corinthians 10:13 NLT

Lord, you are my God;
I will exalt you and praise your name,
for in perfect faithfulness
you have done wonderful things,
things planned long ago.

Isaiah 25:1 NIV

The word of the Lord is upright,
and all his work is done in faithfulness.

Psalm 33:4 ESV

The steadfast love of the Lord never ceases;
his mercies never come to an end;
they are new every morning;
great is your faithfulness.

Lamentations 3:22–23 ESV

I will sing of the Lord's great love forever;
with my mouth I will make your faithfulness known
through all generations.
I will declare that your love stands firm forever,
that you have established your faithfulness in heaven itself.

Psalm 89:1–2 NIV

Fear

Don't be afraid, for I am with you.
Don't be discouraged, for I am your God.
I will strengthen you and help you.
I will hold you up with my victorious right hand.

Isaiah 41:10 NLT

The name of the LORD is a strong tower;
The righteous runs into it and is safe.

Proverbs 18:10 NASB

God is our refuge and strength,
an ever-present help in trouble.

Psalm 46:1 NIV

God has not given us a spirit of fear, but of power and of
love and of a sound mind.

2 Timothy 1:7 NKJV

There is no room in love for fear. Well-formed love banishes
fear. Since fear is crippling, a fearful life—fear of death, fear
of judgment—is one not yet fully formed in love.

1 John 4:18 MSG

The LORD is my light and my salvation;
whom shall I fear?
The LORD is the stronghold of my life;
of whom shall I be afraid?

Psalm 27:1 ESV

When you lie down, you will not be afraid;
when you lie down, your sleep will be sweet.

Proverbs 3:24 NIV

Finances

My God will meet all your needs according to the
riches of his glory in Christ Jesus.

Philippians 4:19 NIV

"Whoever wishes to save his life will lose it; but whoever
loses his life for My sake will find it. For what will it profit
a man if he gains the whole world and forfeits his soul?
Or what will a man give in exchange for his soul?"

Matthew 16:25–26 NASB

Don't love money; be satisfied with what you have.
For God has said, "I will never fail you.
I will never abandon you."

Hebrews 13:5 NLT

As for the rich in this present age, charge them not to
be haughty, nor to set their hopes on the uncertainty
of riches, but on God, who richly provides us with
everything to enjoy.

1 Timothy 6:17 ESV

With me are riches and honor,
enduring wealth and prosperity.
My fruit is better than fine gold;
what I yield surpasses choice silver.
I walk in the way of righteousness,
along the paths of justice,
bestowing a rich inheritance on those who love me
and making their treasuries full.

Proverbs 8:18–21 NIV

Flexibility

Blessed the woman, who listens to me,
awake and ready for me each morning,
alert and responsive as I start my day's work.
When you find me, you find life, real life,
to say nothing of GOD's good pleasure.

Proverbs 8:34–35 MSG

Accept other believers...and don't argue with them
about what they think is right or wrong. For instance...
those who worship the Lord on a special day do it to
honor him. Those who eat any kind of food do so to
honor the Lord, since they give thanks to God before
eating. And those who refuse to eat certain foods also
want to please the Lord and give thanks to God.

Romans 14:1–2, 6 NLT

I know how to be brought low, and I know how to abound.
In any and every circumstance, I have learned the secret of
facing plenty and hunger, abundance and need. I can do
all things through him who strengthens me.

Philippians 4:12–13 ESV

"I prefer a flexible heart to an inflexible ritual."

Matthew 12:7 MSG

You are our Father;
We are the clay, and You our potter;
And all we are the work of Your hand.

Isaiah 64:8 NKJV

Forgiveness

If we confess our sins, He is faithful and just to forgive us our sins and to cleanse us from all unrighteousness.

1 John 1:9 NKJV

"If you forgive other people when they sin against you, your heavenly Father will also forgive you."

Matthew 6:14 NIV

He is so rich in kindness and grace that he purchased our freedom with the blood of his Son and forgave our sins.

Ephesians 1:7 NLT

"Her sins—and they are many—have been forgiven, so she has shown me much love. But a person who is forgiven little shows only little love."

Luke 7:47 NLT

As far as the east is from the west,
So far has He removed our transgressions from us.

Psalm 103:12 NASB

"Whenever you stand praying, forgive, if you have anything against anyone, so that your Father also who is in heaven may forgive you."

Mark 11:25 ESV

You, Lord, are good, and ready to forgive,
And abundant in mercy to all those who call upon You.

Psalm 86:5 NKJV

Friendship

"Greater love has no one than this: to lay down one's life for one's friends. You are my friends if you do what I command. I no longer call you servants, because a servant does not know his master's business. Instead, I have called you friends, for everything that I learned from my Father I have made known to you."

John 15:13–15 NIV

There are "friends" who pretend to be friends, but there is a friend who sticks closer than a brother.

Proverbs 18:24 TLB

A friend loves at all times.

Proverbs 17:17 NKJV

Love prospers when a fault is forgiven, but dwelling on it separates close friends.

Proverbs 17:9 NLT

The right word at the right time
is like a custom-made piece of jewelry,
And a wise friend's timely reprimand
is like a gold ring slipped on your finger.
Reliable friends who do what they say
are like cool drinks in sweltering heat—refreshing!

Proverbs 25:12–13 MSG

"Do to others whatever you would like them to do to you. This is the essence of all that is taught in the law and the prophets."

Matthew 7:12 NLT

Generosity

It is more blessed to give than to receive.

Acts 20:35 NIV

One person gives freely, yet gains even more;
another withholds unduly, but comes to poverty.
A generous person will prosper;
whoever who refreshes others will be refreshed.

Proverbs 11:24–25 NIV

Let each one give as he purposes in his heart, not grudgingly
or of necessity; for God loves a cheerful giver.

2 Corinthians 9:7 NKJV

Whoever is generous to the poor lends to the LORD,
and he will repay him for his deed.

Proverbs 19:17 ESV

"When you give to the needy, do not let your left hand know
what your right hand is doing, so that your giving may be in
secret. Then your Father, who sees what is done in secret,
will reward you."

Matthew 6:3–4 NIV

You shall generously give to him, and your heart shall not
be grieved when you give to him, because for this thing the
LORD your God will bless you in all your work and in all your
undertakings.

Deuteronomy 15:10 NASB

The generous will themselves be blessed,
for they share their food with the poor.

Proverbs 22:9 NIV

Gentleness

It is not fancy hair, gold jewelry, or fine clothes that should make you beautiful. No, your beauty should come from within you—the beauty of a gentle and quiet spirit that will never be destroyed and is very precious to God.

1 Peter 3:3-4 NCV

A gentle answer turns away wrath,
but a harsh word stirs up anger.

Proverbs 15:1 NIV

"Take my yoke upon you, and learn from me, for I am gentle and lowly in heart, and you will find rest for your souls."

Matthew 11:29 ESV

The wisdom that is from above is first pure, then peaceable, gentle, willing to yield, full of mercy and good fruits, without partiality and without hypocrisy.

James 3:17 NKJV

He tends his flock like a shepherd:
He gathers the lambs in his arms
and carries them close to his heart;
he gently leads those that have young.

Isaiah 40:11 NIV

"Blessed are the gentle, for they shall inherit the earth."

Matthew 5:5 NASB

Goodness

Taste and see that the LORD is good;
blessed is the one who takes refuge in him.

Psalm 34:8 NIV

Everything God created is good, and nothing is to be
rejected if it is received with thanksgiving.

1 Timothy 4:4 NIV

The LORD is good to all,
and his mercy is over all that he has made.

Psalm 145:9 ESV

How great is the goodness
you have stored up for those who fear you.
You lavish it on those who come to you for protection,
blessing them before the watching world.

Psalm 31:19 NLT

Work with enthusiasm, as though you were working for the
Lord rather than for people. Remember that the Lord will
reward each one of us for the good we do.

Ephesians 6:7–8 NLT

Examine everything carefully; hold fast to that which is good;
abstain from every form of evil.

1 Thessalonians 5:21–22 NASB

Praise the LORD!
Oh, give thanks to the LORD, for He is good!
For His mercy endures forever.

Psalm 106:1 NKJV

Grace

Let us then with confidence draw near to the throne of grace, that we may receive mercy and find grace to help in time of need.

Hebrews 4:16 ESV

God is so rich in mercy, and he loved us so much, that even though we were dead because of our sins, he gave us life when he raised Christ from the dead. (It is only by God's grace that you have been saved!)...God saved you by his grace when you believed. And you can't take credit for this; it is a gift from God. Salvation is not a reward for the good things we have done, so none of us can boast about it.

Ephesians 2:4–5, 8–9 NLT

Sin...doesn't, have a chance in competition with the aggressive forgiveness we call *grace*. When it's sin versus grace, grace wins hands down. All sin can do is threaten us with death.... Grace...invites us into life— a life that goes on and on and on, world without end.

Romans 5:20–21 MSG

He gives more grace. Therefore He says:
"God resists the proud,
But gives grace to the humble."

James 4:6 NKJV

Sin shall no longer be your master, because you are not under the law, but under grace.

Romans 6:14 NIV

Grief

May our Lord Jesus Christ himself and God our Father,
who loved us and by his grace gave us eternal comfort
and a wonderful hope, comfort you and strengthen you.

2 Thessalonians 2:16–17 NLT

He turned my sorrow into joy!
He took away my clothes of mourning
and clothed me with joy.

Psalm 30:11 TLB

Those the LORD has rescued will return.
They will enter Zion with singing;
everlasting joy will crown their heads.
Gladness and joy will overtake them,
and sorrow and sighing will flee away.

Isaiah 35:10 NIV

Blessed be the God...of all comfort, who comforts us in
all our tribulation, that we may be able to comfort those
who are in any trouble, with the comfort with which we
ourselves are comforted by God.

2 Corinthians 1:3–4 NKJV

To all who mourn...he will give: beauty for ashes;
joy instead of mourning; praise instead of heaviness.
For God has planted them like strong and
graceful oaks for his own glory.

Isaiah 61:3 TLB

He will once again fill your mouth with laughter
and your lips with shouts of joy.

Job 8:21 NLT

Guidance

Guide me in your truth and teach me,
for you are God my Savior,
and my hope is in you all day long.

Psalm 25:5 NIV

Trust in the LORD with all your heart,
And lean not on your own understanding;
In all your ways acknowledge Him,
And He shall direct your paths.

Proverbs 3:5–6 NKJV

We can make our plans,
but the LORD determines our steps.

Proverbs 16:9 NLT

I will instruct you and teach you in the way you should go;
I will counsel you with my loving eye on you.

Psalm 32:8 NIV

The LORD directs the steps of the godly.
He delights in every detail of their lives.
Though they stumble, they will never fall,
for the LORD holds them by the hand.

Psalm 37:23–24 NLT

Whether you turn to the right or to the left,
your ears will hear a voice behind you, saying,
"This is the way; walk in it."

Isaiah 30:21 NIV

Health

He was pierced for our transgressions,
he was crushed for our iniquities;
the punishment that brought us peace was on him,
and by his wounds we are healed.

Isaiah 53:5 NIV

My child, pay attention to what I say.
Listen carefully to my words.
Don't lose sight of them.
Let them penetrate deep into your heart,
for they bring life to those who find them,
and healing to their whole body.

Proverbs 4:20–22 NLT

"Daughter, your faith has made you well; go in peace
and be healed of your affliction."

Mark 5:34 NASB

A cheerful heart does good like medicine.

Proverbs 17:22 TLB

Trust God from the bottom of your heart;
don't try to figure out everything on your own.
Listen for God's voice in everything you do,
everywhere you go;
he's the one who will keep you on track.
Don't assume that you know it all.
Run to God! Run from evil!
Your body will glow with health,
your very bones will vibrate with life!

Proverbs 3:5–8 MSG

Helpfulness

Carry each other's burdens, and in this way you will fulfill the law of Christ.... As we have opportunity, let us do good to all people.

Galatians 6:2, 10 NIV

"Who is the greater, one who reclines at table or one who serves? Is it not the one who reclines at table? But I am among you as the one who serves."

Luke 22:27 ESV

Give generously, for your gifts will return to you later. Divide your gifts among many, for in the days ahead you yourself may need much help.

Ecclesiastes 11:1–2 TLB

Let the message about Christ, in all its richness, fill your lives. Teach and counsel each other with all the wisdom he gives. Sing psalms and hymns and spiritual songs to God with thankful hearts. And whatever you do or say, do it as a representative of the Lord Jesus, giving thanks through him to God the Father.

Colossians 3:16–17 NLT

God has given each of you a gift from his great variety of spiritual gifts. Use them well to serve one another.

1 Peter 4:10–11 NLT

"Even the Son of Man did not come to be served, but to serve, and to give His life a ransom for many."

Mark 10:45 NKJV

Honesty

Speaking the truth in love, we will grow to become in every respect the mature body of him who is the head, that is, Christ.

Ephesians 4:15 NIV

Putting away lying, "Let each one of you speak truth with his neighbor," for we are members of one another.

Ephesians 4:25 NKJV

Truthful words stand the test of time,
but lies are soon exposed.

Proverbs 12:19 NLT

Do not lie to one another, since you laid aside the old self with its evil practices, and have put on the new self who is being renewed to a true knowledge.

Colossians 3:9-10 NASB

Good people who live honest lives
will be a blessing to their children.

Proverbs 20:7 NCV

A good name is to be chosen rather than great riches,
Loving favor rather than silver and gold.

Proverbs 22:1 NKJV

The Lord detests lying lips,
but he delights in people who are trustworthy.

Proverbs 12:22 NIV

Honor

Those who honor me I will honor.

1 Samuel 2:30 NIV

Humble yourselves under the mighty power of God,
and at the right time he will lift you up in honor.

1 Peter 5:6 NLT

We want to live honorably in everything we do.

Hebrews 13:18 NLT

A gracious woman retains honor.

Proverbs 11:16 NKJV

Love one another with mutual affection;
outdo one another in showing honor.

Romans 12:10 NRSV

Whoever pursues righteousness and love
finds life, prosperity and honor.

Proverbs 21:21 NIV

"My Father will honor the one who serves me."

John 12:26 NIV

Let us be grateful for receiving a kingdom that cannot
be shaken, and thus let us offer to God acceptable
worship, with reverence and awe.

Hebrews 12:28 ESV

We are careful to be honorable before the Lord, but we
also want everyone else to see that we are honorable.

2 Corinthians 8:21 NLT

Hope

We can rejoice, too, when we run into problems and trials, for we know that they help us develop endurance. And endurance develops strength of character, and character strengthens our confident hope of salvation. And this hope will not lead to disappointment. For we know how dearly God loves us, because he has given us the Holy Spirit to fill our hearts with his love.

Romans 5:3–5 NLT

Blessed be the God and Father of our Lord Jesus Christ! According to his great mercy, he has caused us to be born again to a living hope through the resurrection of Jesus Christ.

1 Peter 1:3 ESV

May the God of hope fill you with all joy and peace as you trust in him, so that you may overflow with hope by the power of the Holy Spirit.

Romans 15:13 NIV

GOD...rekindles burned-out lives with fresh hope, Restoring dignity and respect to their lives— a place in the sun!

1 Samuel 2:7–8 MSG

The LORD is good to those whose hope is in him, to the one who seeks him.

Lamentations 3:25 NIV

Humility

In your relationships with one another,
have the same mindset as Christ Jesus:
Who, being in very nature God,
did not consider equality with God something
to be used to his own advantage;
rather, he made himself nothing
by taking the very nature of a servant,
being made in human likeness.
And being found in appearance as a man,
he humbled himself
by becoming obedient to death—
even death on a cross!
Therefore God exalted him to the highest place
and gave him the name that is above every name.

Philippians 2:5–9 NIV

Be content with who you are, and don't put on airs.
God's strong hand is on you; he'll promote you at the right time.
Live carefree before God; he is most careful with you.

1 Peter 5:6–7 MSG

Humble yourselves in the sight of the Lord, and He will lift you up.

James 4:10 NKJV

The LORD has told you what is good,
and this is what he requires of you:
to do what is right, to love mercy,
and to walk humbly with your God.

Micah 6:8 NLT

Inspiration

"You are the light of the world. A city set on a hill cannot be hidden. Nor do people light a lamp and put it under a basket, but on a stand, and it gives light to all in the house. In the same way, let your light shine before others, so that they may see your good works and give glory to your Father who is in heaven."

Matthew 5:14–16 ESV

The precepts of the LORD are right,
giving joy to the heart.
The commands of the LORD are radiant,
giving light to the eyes.

Psalm 19:8 NIV

Your laws are my treasure; they are my heart's delight.

Psalm 119:111 NLT

Pursue a righteous life—a life of wonder, faith, love, steadiness, courtesy. Run hard and fast in the faith. Seize the eternal life, the life you were called to, the life you so fervently embraced in the presence of so many witnesses.

1 Timothy 6:11–12 MSG

"I am the Light of the world; he who follows Me will not walk in the darkness, but will have the Light of life."

John 8:12 NASB

Integrity

You test the heart and are pleased with integrity. All these things I have given willingly and with honest intent.

> 1 Chronicles 29:17 NIV

People with integrity walk safely,
but those who follow crooked paths will slip and fall.

> Proverbs 10:9 NLT

Be careful to do what is right in the eyes of everyone.

> Romans 12:17 NIV

Vindicate me, O Lord,
for I have walked in my integrity,
and I have trusted in the Lord without wavering.
…I shall walk in my integrity;
redeem me, and be gracious to me.

> Psalm 26:1, 11 ESV

The integrity of the upright will guide them,
But the crookedness of the treacherous will destroy them.

> Proverbs 11:3 NASB

The righteous walk in integrity—
happy are the children who follow them!

> Proverbs 20:7 NRSV

Because of my integrity you uphold me
and set me in your presence forever.

> Psalm 41:12 NIV

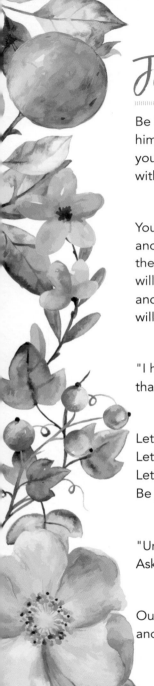

Joy

Be truly glad! There is wonderful joy ahead.... You love him even though you have never seen him. Though you do not see him now, you trust him; and you rejoice with a glorious, inexpressible joy.

1 Peter 1:6, 8 NLT

You will go out in joy
and be led forth in peace;
the mountains and hills
will burst into song before you,
and all the trees of the field
will clap their hands.

Isaiah 55:12 NIV

"I have told you this so that my joy may be in you and that your joy may be complete."

John 15:11 NIV

Let all those rejoice who put their trust in You;
Let them ever shout for joy, because You defend them;
Let those also who love Your name
Be joyful in You.

Psalm 5:11 NKJV

"Until now you have not asked for anything in my name. Ask and you will receive, and your joy will be complete."

John 16:24 NIV

Our mouth was filled with laughter,
and our tongue with shouts of joy.

Psalm 126:2 ESV

Justice

He will not judge by appearance, false evidence,
or hearsay, but will defend the poor and the exploited.
He will rule against the wicked who oppress them.
For he will be clothed with fairness and with truth.

Isaiah 11:3–5 TLB

The LORD secures justice for the poor
and upholds the cause of the needy.

Psalm 140:12 NIV

Righteousness and justice
are the foundation of Your throne.

Psalm 89:14 NKJV

Beloved, do not avenge yourselves, but rather give
place to wrath; for it is written, "Vengeance is Mine,
I will repay," says the Lord.

Romans 12:19 NKJV

Seek justice, correct oppression;
bring justice to the fatherless,
plead the widow's cause.

Isaiah 1:17 ESV

To do what is right and just
is more acceptable to the LORD than sacrifice.

Proverbs 21:3 NIV

He did not retaliate when he was insulted, nor threaten
revenge when he suffered. He left his case in the hands
of God, who always judges fairly.

1 Peter 2:23 NLT

Kindness

"Love your enemies, do good to them, and lend to them without expecting to get anything back. Then your reward will be great, and you will be children of the Most High."

Luke 6:35 NIV

When she speaks, her words are wise,
and she gives instructions with kindness.

Proverbs 31:26 NLT

How does God's love abide in anyone who has the world's goods and sees a brother or sister in need and yet refuses help? Little children, let us love, not in word or speech, but in truth and action.

1 John 3:17–18 NRSV

Do you presume on the riches of his kindness and forbearance and patience, not knowing that God's kindness is meant to lead you to repentance?

Romans 2:4 ESV

I will tell of the kindnesses of the LORD,
the deeds for which he is to be praised,
according to all the LORD has done for us...
according to his compassion and many kindnesses.

Isaiah 63:7 NIV

His merciful kindness is great toward us,
And the truth of the LORD endures forever.
Praise the LORD!

Psalm 117:2 NKJV

Loneliness

The LORD is near to all who call on him,
to all who call on him in truth.

Psalm 145:18 NIV

O LORD, You have searched me and known me.
You know my sitting down and my rising up;
You understand my thought afar off.
You comprehend my path and my lying down,
And are acquainted with all my ways.
For there is not a word on my tongue,
But behold, O LORD, You know it altogether.

Psalm 139:1–4 NKJV

Turn to me and have mercy,
for I am alone and in deep distress.

Psalm 25:16 NLT

I am sure that neither death nor life, nor angels nor
rulers, nor things present nor things to come, nor
powers, nor height nor depth, nor anything else in all
creation, will be able to separate us from the love of
God in Christ Jesus our Lord.

Romans 8:38–39 ESV

By this we know that we abide in Him and He in us,
because He has given us of His Spirit.

1 John 4:13 NASB

"Behold, I am with you always, to the end of the age."

Matthew 28:20 ESV

Loss

God's dwelling place is now among the people, and he will dwell with them. They will be his people, and God himself will be with them and be their God. He will wipe every tear from their eyes. There will be no more death or mourning or crying or pain, for the old order of things has passed away.

Revelation 21:3–4 NIV

May your unfailing love be my comfort,
according to your promise to your servant.

Psalm 119:76 NIV

Those who sow in tears
shall reap with shouts of joy!

Psalm 126:5 ESV

"Come to me, all you who are weary and burdened, and I will give you rest. Take my yoke upon you and learn from me, for I am gentle and humble in heart, and you will find rest for your souls."

Matthew 11:28–29 NIV

Unless the LORD had helped me,
I would soon have settled in the silence of the grave.
I cried out, "I am slipping!"
but your unfailing love, O LORD, supported me.
When doubts filled my mind,
your comfort gave me renewed hope and cheer.

Psalm 94:17–19 NLT

Love

Satisfy us in the morning with your unfailing love,
that we may sing for joy and be glad all our days.

Psalm 90:14 NIV

Three things will last forever—faith, hope, and love—
and the greatest of these is love.

1 Corinthians 13:13 NLT

"This is how much God loved the world: He gave his
Son, his one and only Son. And this is why: so that no
one need be destroyed; by believing in him, anyone can
have a whole and lasting life."

John 3:16 MSG

Know therefore that the LORD your God is God;
he is the faithful God, keeping his covenant of love
to a thousand generations of those who love him
and keep his commandments.

Deuteronomy 7:9 NIV

Let love be without hypocrisy. Abhor what is evil.
Cling to what is good. Be kindly affectionate to one
another with brotherly love.

Romans 12:9–10 NKJV

Let love and faithfulness never leave you;
bind them around your neck,
write them on the tablet of your heart.

Proverbs 3:3 NIV

Patience

They who wait for the Lord
shall renew their strength;
they shall mount up with wings like eagles;
they shall run and not be weary;
they shall walk and not faint.

Isaiah 40:31 ESV

Have unity of spirit, sympathy, love for one another, a tender heart, and a humble mind. Do not repay evil for evil or abuse for abuse; but, on the contrary, repay with a blessing. It is for this that you were called—that you might inherit a blessing.

1 Peter 3:8–9 NRSV

Follow the example of those who are going to inherit God's promises because of their faith and endurance.

Hebrews 6:12 NLT

Make me truly happy by agreeing wholeheartedly with each other, loving one another, and working together with one mind and purpose.

Philippians 2:2 NLT

Live in harmony with one another. Do not be proud, but be willing to associate with people of low position. Do not be conceited.

Romans 12:16 NIV

Rest in the Lord and wait patiently for Him....
Those who wait for the Lord, they will inherit the land.

Psalm 37:7–9 NASB

Peace

"Peace I leave with you; my peace I give you. I do not give to you as the world gives. Do not let your hearts be troubled and do not be afraid."

John 14:27 NIV

"These things I have spoken to you, so that in Me you may have peace. In the world you have tribulation, but take courage; I have overcome the world."

John 16:33 NASB

If people's thinking is controlled by the sinful self, there is death. But if their thinking is controlled by the Spirit, there is life and peace.

Romans 8:6 NCV

God is not a God of confusion but of peace.

1 Corinthians 14:33 NASB

Let the peace of Christ rule in your hearts, since as members of one body you were called to peace.

Colossians 3:15 NIV

Those who love your instructions have great peace and do not stumble.

Psalm 119:165 NLT

May the Lord of peace himself give you peace at all times and in every way. The Lord be with all of you.

2 Thessalonians 3:16 NIV

Perseverance

Consider it pure joy...whenever you face trials of many kinds, because you know that the testing of your faith develops perseverance. Perseverance must finish its work so that you may be mature and complete, not lacking anything.

James 1:2–4 NIV

God blesses those who patiently endure testing and temptation. Afterward they will receive the crown of life that God has promised to those who love him.

James 1:12 NLT

Let us not grow weary of doing good, for in due season we will reap, if we do not give up.

Galatians 6:9 ESV

Since we are surrounded by such a great cloud of witnesses, let us throw off everything that hinders and the sin that so easily entangles. And let us run with perseverance the race marked out for us, fixing our eyes on Jesus. ...so that you will not grow weary and lose heart.

Hebrews 12:1–3 NIV

May the Lord direct your hearts into God's love and Christ's perseverance.

2 Thessalonians 3:5 NIV

Praise

Praise the LORD!
Praise God in his sanctuary;
praise him in his mighty heavens!
Praise him for his mighty deeds;
praise him according to his excellent greatness!...
Let everything that has breath praise the LORD!

Psalm 150:1–2, 6 ESV

Let us continually offer the sacrifice of praise to God,
that is, the fruit of our lips, giving thanks to His name.

Hebrews 13:15 NKJV

O LORD, You are my God.
I will exalt You,
I will praise Your name,
For You have done wonderful things.

Isaiah 25:1 NKJV

Praise the LORD from the heavens;
praise him in the heights above.
Praise him, all his angels;
praise him, all his heavenly hosts.
Praise him, sun and moon;
praise him, all you shining stars.
Praise him, you highest heavens
and you waters above the skies.
Let them praise the name of the LORD,
for at his command they were created.

Psalm 148:1–5 NIV

Prayer

"Ask and it will be given to you; seek and you will find; knock and the door will be opened to you. For everyone who asks receives; he who seeks finds; and to him who knocks, the door will be opened."

Matthew 7:7–8 NIV

My voice You shall hear in the morning, O LORD;
In the morning I will direct it to You,
And I will look up.

Psalm 5:3 NKJV

Confess your sins to each other and pray for each other so that you may be healed. The prayer of a righteous person is powerful and effective.

James 5:16 NIV

Pray about everything. Tell God what you need, and thank him for all he has done.

Philippians 4:6 NLT

The Spirit also helps our weakness; for we do not know how to pray as we should, but the Spirit Himself intercedes for us with groanings too deep for words.

Romans 8:26 NASB

You, God, are my God, earnestly I seek you;
I thirst for you, my whole being longs for you,
in a dry and parched land where there is no water.

Psalm 63:1 NIV

Pray without ceasing.

1 Thessalonians 5:17 NKJV

Promises

Your promises have been thoroughly tested,
and your servant loves them.
…My eyes stay open through the watches of the night,
that I may meditate on your promises.

Psalm 119:140, 148 NIV

Not one word of all the good words which the LORD
your God spoke concerning you has failed; all have
been fulfilled for you, not one of them has failed.

Joshua 23:14 NASB

To him who is able to do immeasurably more than all we
ask or imagine, according to his power that is at work
within us, to him be glory...for ever and ever! Amen.

Ephesians 3:20–21 NIV

The LORD always keeps his promises;
he is gracious in all he does.

Psalm 145:13 NLT

He has granted to us his precious and very great promises,
so that through them you may become partakers of the
divine nature, having escaped from the corruption that is in
the world.

2 Peter 1:3-4 ESV

All of God's promises have been fulfilled in Christ with a
resounding "Yes!"

2 Corinthians 1:20 NLT

Purpose

Live as citizens of heaven, conducting yourselves in a manner worthy of the Good News about Christ... standing together with one spirit and one purpose, fighting together for the faith. Don't be intimidated in any way by your enemies. This will be a sign to them that you are going to be saved, even by God himself.

Philippians 1:27–28 NLT

Be attentive to my words;
incline your ear to my sayings.
Let them not escape from your sight;
keep them within your heart.
Let your eyes look directly forward,
and your gaze be straight before you.

Proverbs 4:20–21, 25 ESV

If you're serious about living this new resurrection life with Christ, *act* like it. Pursue the things over which Christ presides. Don't shuffle along, eyes to the ground, absorbed with the things right in front of you. Look up, and be alert to what is going on around Christ—that's where the action is. See things from *his* perspective.

Colossians 3:1–2 MSG

We know that all things work together for good to those who love God, to those who are the called according to His purpose.

Romans 8:28 NKJV

Reconciliation

We have stopped evaluating others from a human point of view. At one time we thought of Christ merely from a human point of view. How differently we know him now! This means that anyone who belongs to Christ has become a new person. The old life is gone; a new life has begun! And all of this is a gift from God, who brought us back to himself through Christ. And God has given us this task of reconciling people to him.

2 Corinthians 5:16–18 NLT

You were separate from Christ...foreigners to the covenants of the promise, without hope and without God in the world. But now in Christ Jesus you who once were far away have been brought near.

Ephesians 2:12–13 NIV

God put the world square with himself through the Messiah, giving the world a fresh start by offering forgiveness of sins. God has given us the task of telling everyone what he is doing. We're Christ's representatives. God uses us to persuade men and women to drop their differences and enter into God's work of making things right between them. We're speaking for Christ himself now: Become friends with God; he's already a friend with you.

2 Corinthians 5:19–20 MSG

Relationships

Two are better than one,
because they have a good return for their labor:
If either of them falls down,
one can help the other up.

Ecclesiastes 4:9–10 NIV

Perfume and incense bring joy to the heart,
and the pleasantness of a friend
springs from their heartfelt advice.

Proverbs 27:9 NIV

Love each other with genuine affection,
and take delight in honoring each other.

Romans 12:10 NLT

Above all else, guard your heart,
for everything you do flows from it.

Proverbs 4:23 NIV

As those who have been chosen of God, holy and beloved,
put on a heart of compassion, kindness, humility, gentleness
and patience; bearing with one another, and forgiving each
other, whoever has a complaint against anyone; just as the
Lord forgave you, so also should you. Beyond all these
things put on love, which is the perfect bond of unity.

Colossians 3:12–14 NASB

As iron sharpens iron,
so a friend sharpens a friend.

Proverbs 27:17 NLT

Reliability

Every good and perfect gift is from above, coming down from the Father of the heavenly lights, who does not change like shifting shadows.

James 1:17 NIV

You are near, LORD,
and all your commands are true.
Long ago I learned from your statutes
that you established them to last forever.

Psalm 119:151–152 NIV

The grass withers, And its flower falls away,
But the word of the LORD endures forever.

1 Peter 1:24–25 NKJV

"One who is faithful in a very little is also faithful in much."

Luke 16:10 ESV

With all my heart I have sought You;
Do not let me wander from Your commandments.
Your word I have treasured in my heart,
That I may not sin against You.
…Teach me, O LORD, the way of Your statutes,
And I shall observe it to the end.

Psalm 119:10–11, 33 NASB

Watch yourselves, so that you may not lose what we have worked for, but may win a full reward.

2 John 1:8 ESV

Respect

Do nothing out of selfish ambition or vain conceit. Rather, in humility value others above yourselves, not looking to your own interests but each of you to the interests of the others.

Philippians 2:3–4 NIV

For the Lord's sake, yield to the people who have authority in this world.... It is God's desire that by doing good you should stop foolish people from saying stupid things about you. Live as free people, but do not use your freedom as an excuse to do evil. Live as servants of God. Show respect for all people: Love the brothers and sisters of God's family.

1 Peter 2:13, 15–17 NCV

Have confidence in your leaders and submit to their authority, because they keep watch over you as those who must give an account. Do this so that their work will be a joy, not a burden, for that would be of no benefit to you.

Hebrews 13:17 NIV

Appreciate those who diligently labor among you, and have charge over you in the Lord and give you instruction...esteem them very highly in love because of their work. Live in peace with one another.

1 Thessalonians 5:12–13 NASB

Self-control

The grace of God has appeared that offers salvation to all people. It teaches us to say "No" to ungodliness and worldly passions, and to live self-controlled, upright and godly lives in this present age.

Titus 2:11-12 NIV

Set a guard over my mouth, LORD;
keep watch over the door of my lips.
Do not let my heart be drawn to what is evil.

Psalm 141:3-4 NIV

Prepare your minds for action, keep sober in spirit, fix your hope completely on the grace to be brought to you at the revelation of Jesus Christ.

1 Peter 1:13 NASB

This is the will of God, your sanctification… that each one of you know how to control your own body in holiness and honor.

1 Thessalonians 4:3-4 NRSV

The end of all things is at hand; therefore be self-controlled and sober-minded for the sake of your prayers.

1 Peter 4:7 ESV

We all make many mistakes. For if we could control our tongues, we would be perfect and could also control ourselves in every other way.

James 3:2 NLT

You were once darkness, but now you are light in the Lord. Live as children of light.

Ephesians 5:8 NIV

Serving

Each of you should use whatever gift you have received to serve others, as faithful stewards of God's grace in its various forms. If anyone serves, they should do so with the strength God provides, so that in all things God may be praised through Jesus Christ.

1 Peter 4:10–11 NIV

"He who is greatest among you, let him be as the younger, and he who governs as he who serves. For who is greater, he who sits at the table, or he who serves? Is it not he who sits at the table? Yet I am among you as the One who serves."

Luke 22:26–27 NKJV

"Do you want to stand out? Then step down. Be a servant. If you puff yourself up, you'll get the wind knocked out of you. But if you're content to simply be yourself, your life will count for plenty."

Matthew 23:11–12 MSG

"Even the Son of Man did not come to be served, but to serve, and to give His life a ransom for many."

Mark 10:45 NASB

You have been called to live in freedom, my brothers and sisters. But don't use your freedom to satisfy your sinful nature. Instead, use your freedom to serve one another in love.

Galatians 5:13 NLT

Sickness

The righteous person faces many troubles,
but the Lord comes to the rescue each time.

Psalm 34:19 NLT

Have you never heard?
Have you never understood?
The Lord is the everlasting God,
the Creator of all the earth.
He never grows weak or weary.
No one can measure the depths of his understanding.
He gives power to the weak
and strength to the powerless.

Isaiah 40:28-29 NLT

Let us therefore come boldly to the throne of grace, that we
may obtain mercy and find grace to help in time of need.

Hebrews 4:16 NKJV

My flesh and my heart may fail,
but God is the strength of my heart
and my portion forever.

Psalm 73:26 NIV

Blessed be the Lord,
Because He has heard the voice of my supplication.
The Lord is my strength and my shield;
My heart trusts in Him, and I am helped;
Therefore my heart exults,
And with my song I shall thank Him.

Psalm 28:6-7 NASB

Stress

Blessed is the one who trusts in the LORD,
whose confidence is in him.
They will be like a tree planted by the water
that sends out its roots by the stream.
It does not fear when heat comes;
its leaves are always green.
It has no worries in a year of drought
and never fails to bear fruit.

Jeremiah 17:7–8 NIV

"Give your entire attention to what God is doing right now, and don't get worked up about what may or may not happen tomorrow. God will help you deal with whatever hard things come up when the time comes."

Matthew 6:34 MSG

Commit your actions to the LORD,
and your plans will succeed.

Proverbs 16:3 NLT

The LORD also will be a refuge...in times of trouble.
Those who know Your name will put their trust in You;
For You, LORD, have not forsaken those who seek You.

Psalm 9:9–10 NKJV

May the God who gives endurance and encouragement give you the same attitude of mind toward each other that Christ Jesus had.

Romans 15:5 NIV

Thankfulness

Enter his gates with thanksgiving,
and his courts with praise!
Give thanks to him; bless his name!
For the LORD is good;
his steadfast love endures forever,
and his faithfulness to all generations.

Psalm 100:4–5 ESV

Rejoice always, pray without ceasing, in everything
give thanks; for this is the will of God.

1 Thessalonians 5:16–18 NKJV

Give thanks to the LORD, for he is good; his love
endures forever.

1 Chronicles 16:34 NIV

Let us come into his presence with thanksgiving;
let us make a joyful noise to him with songs of praise!

Psalm 95:2 ESV

Let us continually offer up a sacrifice of praise to God,
that is, the fruit of lips that give thanks to His name.

Hebrews 13:15 NASB

We give thanks to God always for you, making mention
of you in our prayers; constantly bearing in mind your
work of faith and labor of love and steadfastness of hope.

1 Thessalonians 1:2–3 NASB

Trust

The LORD is my strength and my shield;
my heart trusts in him, and he helps me.

Psalm 28:7 NIV

May your whole self—spirit, soul, and body—
be kept safe and without fault when our
Lord Jesus Christ comes. You can trust the One
who calls you to do that for you.

1 Thessalonians 5:23–24 NCV

Those who know Your name will put their trust in You;
For You, LORD, have not forsaken those who seek You.

Psalm 9:10 NKJV

God's way is perfect.
All the LORD's promises prove true.
He is a shield for all who look to him for protection.
For who is God except the LORD?
Who but our God is a solid rock?

Psalm 18:30–31 NLT

God, the source of hope, will fill you completely
with joy and peace because you trust in him.
Then you will overflow with confident hope
through the power of the Holy Spirit.

Romans 15:13 NLT

Trustworthiness

I keep my eyes always on the LORD.
With him at my right hand, I will not be shaken.

Psalm 16:8 NIV

A gossip goes around telling secrets,
but those who are trustworthy can keep a confidence.

Proverbs 11:13 NLT

Show yourself in all respects to be a model of good works,
and in your teaching show integrity, dignity, and sound
speech that cannot be condemned, so that an opponent
may be put to shame, having nothing evil to say about us.

Titus 2:7-8 ESV

"Until heaven and earth disappear, not the smallest letter,
not the least stroke of a pen, will be any means disappear
from the Law until everything is accomplished."

Matthew 5:18 NIV

The works of his hands are faithful and just;
all his precepts are trustworthy.

Psalm 111:7 NRSV

The law of the LORD is perfect,
refreshing the soul.
The statutes of the LORD are trustworthy,
making wise the simple.

Psalm 19:7 NIV

Truth

Teach me your ways, O Lord,
that I may live according to your truth!
Grant me purity of heart,
so that I may honor you.

Psalm 86:11 NLT

"When he, the Spirit of truth, comes,
he will guide you into all the truth."

John 16:13 NIV

The very essence of your words is truth;
all your just regulations will stand forever.

Psalm 119:160 NLT

Jesus said, "If you hold to my teaching, you are really
my disciples. Then you will know the truth, and the
truth will set you free."

John 8:31–32 NIV

You desire truth in the innermost being,
And in the hidden part You will make me know wisdom.

Psalm 51:6 NASB

Truthful words stand the test of time,
but lies are soon exposed.

Proverbs 12:19 NLT

Let us not love with words or speech but with actions
and in truth.

1 John 3:18 NIV

148

Understanding

The unfolding of your words gives light;
it gives understanding to the simple.

Psalm 119:130 NIV

Listen carefully to wisdom;
set your mind on understanding.
Cry out for wisdom,
and beg for understanding.
Search for it like silver,
and hunt for it like hidden treasure.
Then you will understand respect for the LORD,
and you will find that you know God.

Proverbs 2:2-5 NCV

Blessed is the one who finds wisdom,
and the one who gets understanding.

Proverbs 3:13 ESV

What we have received is not the spirit of the world, but the Spirit who is from God, so that we may understand what God has freely given us.

1 Corinthians 2:12 NIV

Be filled with the knowledge of His will in all spiritual wisdom and understanding, so that you will walk in a manner worthy of the Lord… and increasing in the knowledge of God.

Colossians 1:9-10 NASB

Do not be unwise, but understand what the will of the Lord is.

Ephesians 5:17 NKJV

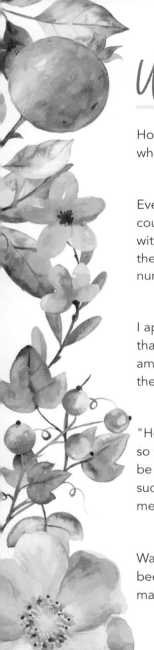

Unity

How good and pleasant it is
when God's people live together in unity!

Psalm 133:1 NIV

Every day they continued to meet together in the temple courts. They broke bread in their homes and ate together with glad and sincere hearts, praising God and enjoying the favor of all the people. And the Lord added to their number daily those who were being saved.

Acts 2:46–47 NIV

I appeal to you…by the name of our Lord Jesus Christ, that all of you agree, and that there be no divisions among you, but that you be united in the same mind and the same judgment.

1 Corinthians 1:10 ESV

"Holy Father…protect them by the power of your name so that they will be united just as we are…that they will all be one, just as you and I are one….May they experience such perfect unity that the world will know that you sent me and that you love them as much as you love me."

John 17:11, 21–23 NLT

Walk in a manner worthy of the calling to which you have been called…bearing with one another in love, eager to maintain the unity of the Spirit in the bond of peace.

Ephesians 4:1–3 ESV

Victory

You can prepare a horse
for the day of battle.
But the power to win
comes from the Lord.

Proverbs 21:31 NIRV

Every child of God defeats this evil world,
and we achieve this victory through our faith.

1 John 5:4 NLT

From the Lord comes deliverance.
May your blessing be on your people.

Psalm 3:8 NIV

"The Lord your God is the one who goes
with you to fight for you against your enemies
to give you victory."

Deuteronomy 20:4 NIV

Wisdom

The wisdom from above is first of all pure. It is also peace loving, gentle at all times, and willing to yield to others. It is full of mercy and good deeds. It shows no favoritism and is always sincere.

James 3:17 NLT

Oh, the depth of the riches both of the wisdom and knowledge of God! How unsearchable are His judgments and unfathomable His ways!

Romans 11:33 NASB

Do not let wisdom and understanding out of your sight, preserve sound judgment and discretion; they will be life for you.

Proverbs 3:21–22 NIV

Blessed are those who find wisdom,
those who gain understanding,
for she is more profitable than silver
and yields better returns than gold.
She is more precious than rubies;
nothing you desire can compare with her.
Long life is in her right hand;
in her left hand are riches and honor.
Her ways are pleasant ways,
and all her paths are peace.

Proverbs 3:13–17 NIV

If any of you lacks wisdom, you should ask God, who gives generously to all without finding fault, and it will be given to you.

James 1:5 NIV

Worry

Don't worry about anything; instead, pray about everything. Tell God what you need, and thank him for all he has done. Then you will experience God's peace, which exceeds anything we can understand. His peace will guard your hearts and minds as you live in Christ Jesus.

Philippians 4:6–7 NLT

"Which of you by worrying can add a single hour to his life's span?"

Luke 12:25 NASB

Worry weighs a person down;
an encouraging word cheers a person up.

Proverbs 12:25 NLT

Give your burdens to the LORD,
and he will take care of you.

Psalm 55:22 NLT

"Do not worry about your life, what you will eat or drink; or about your body, what you will wear. Is not life more than food, and the body more than clothes? Look at the birds of the air; they do not sow or reap or store away in barns, and yet your heavenly Father feeds them. Are you not much more valuable than they?"

Matthew 6:25–26 NIV

May the Lord of peace himself give you peace at all times in every way.

2 Thessalonians 3:16 ESV